GW00721739

Journey of the Beloved Spirit

Kay Santillo

To David and Denise
With much love,
Kay xx

Just Print IT! Publications
HUNTINGDON – ENGLAND

Also by Kay Santillo

Inhaling Bravely on Daylight
The SOD Saga
Six Island Stories
The Medium Sized Book Of Sensitive Health Issue Topics

Published & printed by Just Print IT! Publications
59 The Whaddons, Huntingdon, Cambs., PE18 7NW
Tel: 01480 450880

ISBN 1 902869 20 6

Cover photo:
Garden of the Gods, Colorado Springs, USA

First Edition

Journey of the Beloved Spirit

In March 2000, my life journey led me to Patrick Gamble, to have my spirit guide painted. My guide was a young female spirit, who looked out at me from the canvas with a clear, direct gaze. I felt that her name was Osaka. I welcomed her into my heart and almost immediately felt I should be writing 'things' down.

I had no idea what words would come when I first lit a candle, sat down expectantly with a pen and paper and asked for guidance. It felt as if the first words I wrote came from me, as in the opening of a dialogue, but the reply was instant and felt very encouraging:

Me: *I feel so much the need to connect, to be guided, and I ask that you guide me towards the light – the bright, beckoning light from which all goodness and hope flow.*

Osaka: *When the sky is dark, the light cannot be quenched. Through the love in people's hearts, all the darkness in the world can be banished. Draw together, people of light, and love for the sake of the Earth.*

Why do you worry where these words come from, you or me? The words are important, not their origin. Share the words – share the light.

At first, I just continued to write a couple of sentences or a paragraph at a time, but after a few months, I felt there was going to be more – and thus *Journey of the Beloved Spirit* was born. I enjoyed writing it immensely. I felt as if I was on a higher plane and the energy emanating from the words was so beautiful that I was often moved to tears.

Osaka continues to convey the most wonderful love and encouragement. I hope that this will be a book of encouragement to *you*, no matter where or how your individual life journey leads you!

Kay Santillo, September 2002.

Photos

To David and Denise -
Thank you for welcoming me
into your house of light.

Journey of the
Beloved Spirit

Let us start the journey which has already ended – beyond this place and time, beyond the sky, beyond other skies and other worlds, to infinity. The journey is love and love is infinity.

Beyond your furthest and most intimate dreams, you began as a microcosm of the vast knowledge. You began in peace and acceptance, knowing the journey would take you to the limit of your self – you, the microcosm – you, the beloved spirit.

The greatest and most necessary learning takes place at your limits. If, at the time of our limits, we could only know how beyond there is total love – love of the knowledge – the knowledge which is total love.

You began your journey here in darkness and pain, but beyond the confines of your chosen path, infinity had already welcomed you. Beyond the sky which you now perceive in wonder and the ground which gives you stability, the love-place where you have come from waits for you to grow into your journey's knowledge, on towards the light of total love.

Your chosen companion spirits are all playing their part on your journey. You know your chosen ones – you recognise those whose love of knowledge and knowledge of love resonates with your own.

Your journey is your own growth and your journey is part of others' growth. It is so necessary to love others, for the knowledge and the light to expand and deepen and permeate your own soul.

*Your journey is ever changing,
even as the sky changes from one moment to the next*

Your journey is ever changing, even as the sky changes from one moment to the next. When you look at the sky, remember your place of beginning, where you will return. When you walk along your journey's path, let each step be a prayer of thanks for the precious life you have been given. The precious life which is your chance to love.

Even if you cannot see the sky, or if you cannot walk, your inner self, your soul, walks wherever it chooses and watches the sky with eyes of love. The soul's eyes can never be blinded and the soul always walks in freedom.

Your journey may seem long and arduous, cold and cruel, but it is a gift and will only last for as long as it needs. When you are tired, simply rest – you will not lose any ground. Remember, though, to sing, to dance, to smile, to love, for joy. There is no other journey as precious to you as yours and no one can take away your journey.

Take time to watch the sun rise and set. Breathe the air and experience the world you have chosen to inhabit. It can teach you so much. Feel it with your soul as well as your body. Receive its gift with your spirit, but love with everything you are and everything you know. Love your knowledge of love. It is eternal.

If you feel you have lost direction, cease to worry. Cease to strive. Be at one with where you are and connect with the love deep inside yourself. Protect yourself with the love and be patient. All that will be, will be. Always remember love – the divine love from the love-place of vast knowledge, of which you are a microcosm. You will not always understand, but you will know when and where you should go. Go always in love. Love every step of your journey – for your journey is love.

*

There are many tools you may need for your journey, to sustain you through the mountain passes, the arid desert plains and the thick, suffocating mists. Hope is one of the finest – hope and faith, as steady and strong as the rock of wisdom in your own soul, formed from countless other journeys. The rock will yield and deliver when the time is right.

You may have heard much about the water of life – the love that pours from the skies onto the thirsty, needy land, gathering in streams and rivers, to merge into the sea. Let your heart-loving flow. Be a stream of hope and faith and love that replenishes the dryness of despair. Merge with other streams of life, until the power and beauty of everflowing love-spirit is a joy to planet Earth.

Be steadfast and persistent if needs be. Climb doggedly to the heights, to see the distant perspective. Welcome every sight, sound and scent; every stone in your shoe and every thorn in your soul. Sense all that you can and learn from everything. It will greatly aid your soul's vision.

Be always vigilant. Watch the moon and feel the pull of its rhythms. Regain the Earth knowledge, which was once yours, and send love into all that surrounds you. Even the concrete building and desolate waste ground are worth your love, for love is a miracle and nothing is lost.

Look carefully for the smallest sign. Use every faculty you have; every gift; every cell in your being, to sense the way forward. Listen to the voice in the wind. Listen with your whole self. The path will not always be obvious, but the path is always there and will lead you to the

*The path will not always be obvious,
but the path is always there*

love beyond infinity.

Every spirit of light goes Home – every spark of life, from the aborted embryo to the centenarian. God's mansions are innumerable and full of resting spirits. There is a resting-place for you, where you will be forever loved. Those who love are loved, it is an endless treasure.

Exchange your journey's story with those who would listen and tell you their own story. Are you not all messengers of light – of love beyond this world's comprehension? Bring the message of your self – share the secret of your soul. The love-place will guide you, will call to you and sing to you softly in dreams and visions.

Be courageous. Do not feel you have lost your way, for your life is the way. Do not fear the gathering gloom, the tortuous wind, or the savage electrical storm. Sometimes you may need to lie low, to sit out the storm for a while. At other times, when the storm breaks, be thankful for your human emotion, with its power for potential good. True peace will be yours – peace of spirit at the end of the journey, which is also the beginning.

Gaze at the stars and know you will return to your beginning, but be grounded and mindful of your planet home. Receive the vibrations of global pain and sorrow, bless them with your love and return them with your heart's compassion. So much may be darkness and fear, but one single tear of human empathy and caring can bring relief and comfort. A single shining grain of love amid a desert of darkness and hate will reflect the glory of the light.

Respect your journey's tools, for they will nurture you with all you need. Do not take another's burden, one for which you are not fitted. All that is yours will be given to you.

Walk on, beloved spirit. Grow strong and radiant. Grow in wisdom and beauty. Touch your surroundings with your soul's precious caring. Walk on, with a blessing on your lips and the light of the Divine Creator shining from your eyes.

*

So what of the darkness? The darkness needs to be – it has its purpose, just as the dark places in your soul have their purpose, to ultimately lead you to the most precious love.

Darkness and pain. Darkness and fear. Are they not blessings, which heal and purge and beckon you, weary and trembling, into the great love-place that awaits us all?

Never seek the darkness, but rather let it unfold in your being, like a flower of understanding. Sometimes the unfolding will be sudden and forceful, but more often the unfolding will be a slow insistent ache that grows until you must pluck the flower and crush it inside your heart.

Thus the crushing of the darkness flower is love. So much love is yours – so many gifts born of the darkness. So much learning, to set your spirit free!

Though your own darkness is yours alone, you will never be alone. Angels are watching and loving you with so much joy. No tear is ever shed without the heavenly love-light of angels. No aching heart or desolate mind will ever go unnoticed or unloved. Your spirit will strengthen and your own joy will grow, as your knowledge born of darkness deepens and nurtures you.

Do not dwell in the darkness. Never linger in the shade when you could be welcoming the light. The light is your reward – it is your life, your reason, your everything.

Never linger in the shade
when you could be welcoming the light

When your journey's companions enter their own dark-ness, protect them with your prayers – the projection of your heart-warmth, to surround them with your love. No uttered prayer, or whispered plea, or fervent spirit-wish is ever lost.

When pain and fear would overcome you, seek refuge in your own heart place, the constant core of your being. There you will connect with the light, the love that needs and seeks no understanding. Pain and fear are tools for you to use, but without love, they would use you. Love – love – love will make you strong!

Death is never darkness. Death is light, release and love – another step on your journey. Death, which so many fear, is a loving shift of perception that will take you to where you belong.

When your journey's companions meet death, surround them with your love and thanks for all they have helped to teach you. Let them go with joy – their soul memories, their spirit-print will always live on inside you. You may hear them speaking to you in your heart place, in the dream spaces of your soul. Listen, listen with your heart and all your inner knowing.

The darkness is such a blessing. Do not your dream spaces most often awaken in darkness? So much to find in dreams! So many messages, so much love – you would weep with happiness if you could yet see.

There are those who guide you in the darkness and through the darkness. They cannot take away your darkness, but the light of their love shines deep in your heart and deep in your soul.

Darkness and rest. Darkness and growth. Darkness and light. How would you know light without having known darkness? How would you know joy without having known pain? How would you know the wonderful, absolute certainty of love without having known fear?

The darkness will not last forever. Welcome the darkness, use the darkness, bless the darkness. The dawn of light is coming, beloved spirit, and the miracle of love is more beautiful than the dawn.

*

What about direction? Which path? What to carry with you? So many concerns – and yet your only one concern is love – to find, to follow, to be the loving way. The loving way expands your soul. If the expansion should cause you pain, breathe easily, for the pain will turn to joy and peace and infinite, vibrant love.

If at first you feel this life course has been mapped out for you by expectations, needs, genetics, or responsibilities, there will come a time when you must choose your own way, even if you have to leave all you know. You are only leaving this world's constricting familiarities and heading out towards Home and freedom.

Do not plan too far ahead, so that you spend your energy, your precious life force, on that which will be shown you when the flower of time has matured into fruition. Let the essence of each moment blend into your soul, so that you think not where you move, or how you move, or even whether you move.

You need take nothing on your journey, except that which you carry in your soul. As your journey progresses and your spirit evolves, you will know when it is time to discard what is keeping you from the light. What was once a comfortable skin needs to be cast off with joy. Has not the old skin served you well, but is now restricting you from breathing the cool, delicious air of the dawn of your new understanding?

What if you are attacked on your journey? Love is your great and only protection. It is the strongest force in creation. It is the answer to all the questions you ask on all your journeys – for love *is* the journey.

What if you stumble? Not one faltering step along the cliff path or headlong crashing into the ravine can ever injure your soul. Your soul can only learn, if it so chooses. You may have to stumble so many times before the learning, but there is never a single moment when you are not being guided and loved.

*What if you stumble? Not one faltering step ...
can ever injure your soul*

If you would run for a while, with the wind in your hair and the wild joy of creation coursing through your veins, then run, beloved spirit! But listen to your soul's heartbeat and pace yourself according to your soul's needs.

If others say you should run when you would walk, or

should walk when you would run, bless them with your soul-smile and carry on your way. But always be mindful of others' requests – try to ascertain why they are requesting, rather than what they are requesting.

There are so many levels of journeying – through the body, mind, heart and understanding. Love journeys within love journeys – detours of need, hope and compassion.

When you think you have travelled only backwards, think again! Direction is only a word, but destiny is your path to the love-place! The only ultimate way is towards the light, beckoning you with its radiant truth and beauty.

Do not be concerned whether you are in the right place, following the right light. Light is light is light! Do not think your path is better than others' paths, for no one can step in your footsteps and no one has the same feet. Let your feet breathe – let them savour the earth and the rain, the heat of the day and the coldness of night. Your thoughts are your soul's feet – serve them well, for they serve you well.

Do not force your soul's feet where they would not go. They take you on the path of love, beloved spirit. All paths lead to love, because love is all there is. Love in so many forms. Love as infinite energy, transforming everything back into love.

*

Step bravely into the unknown, wherever your heart leads you. The heart knows where it belongs. The heart cannot be drowned out by this world's noise, in fruitless words and actions, but always beats in love and harmony to its own silent rhythms. Listen – listen – listen to the silent rhythms of your heart!

The heart is wise, using so much of what you may consider negative, to lead you into the positive love-knowledge which you came here to find. The heart always has its reasons, which will ultimately lead to your enlightenment.

Sometimes you may feel as if your heart has been broken. Can a heart be broken? Your heart beats on many rhythmic levels, each level to serve you for your greatest good. Even if at one level, you feel your heart in pain, the deeper level is still beating in unison with the spirit stars shining down from the love-place. The deeper level is love and how can love itself be broken?

Your heart may ache for others, but the compassion of your prayers on their behalf will heal the ache in your own heart, even as it heals the wound in theirs. The heart is such a healing instrument, capable of so much beauty.

What if your heart is heavy, when tears blur your vision and a groan escapes from your soul? Your heart is heavy for a reason – it speaks to you in feelings such as these. The heart may mourn and weep for that which causes pain, but the pain is the learning and the heart will sing for joy because of the learning.

Your heart knows its own levels and throughout each lifetime will seek to experience and understand all. The integration of all the heart's levels is the miraculous dawning of the love-knowledge and the light to guide you Home to the love-place.

... the light to guide you Home to the love-place

Can your heart speak to other hearts? Your heart is never still! Your heart always listens for the silent sound of other hearts, even as you sleep and especially when you dream. Your heart would be one with all hearts, as the universal consciousness of love.

Take time to listen to your heart, to understand its deepest rhythms, which are the essence of your soul. Love your heart, even as your heart loves you and beats so selflessly for you.

What of your mind? Your mind is your heart's greatest friend. A heart and mind working and loving in harmony is a wonder of the universe and causes the spirit world to smile.

Your mind can be the sounding board of your heart – the word place, the working space. Let not your mind lead your heart, but rather let your heart lead your mind.

What of the mind's intellect? It is just a tool you have been given for your journey, one that suits you well. Other mind skills are the same – tools offered in love for you, for your benefit and learning. Use them wisely, for they are capable of so much heart-learning.

What of your body, beloved spirit – your vehicle of movement, experience and expression? The heart and mind can nurture your body so well, always in communication with one another. Listen to your body, as you listen to your heart and mind, but do not revere your body above your heart and mind. Does not the body mingle with the dust when the soul flies in freedom amid galaxies of love?

So much may seem complex on your journey – so much to occupy your heart, mind and body, when you would seek peace for all three. Take comfort, for soul peace is yours when your heart leads the way. Follow your heart, beloved spirit, for the heart always knows its shining destiny of love.

*

Smile as you journey inward to the secret recesses of your soul, where each existence retains its learning for you to reclaim and integrate within your beloved self.

There are so many ways to avoid this inward journey – so many distractions, weaknesses and obstacles. Yet you know, from longings which emanate from your secret recesses, that the only way to the love-heaven is via your inward journey.

What do you fear you might find within your own self? Darkness is only the gateway to light. Pain is merely the prompting to learn. Emptiness is just a temporary pre-cursor to being filled with the exquisite joy of universal love. It is indeed fear itself, dear spirit, that needs to be conquered. Do you not think that your self exists for your own benefit? Does not sweet reason lend itself to the understanding that you are your own best friend? Let yourself be your own best friend!

When you feel fear, remember that just as light is stronger than darkness, so love is stronger than fear – and love is all around you. It is in the rising sap and the decaying vegetation of nature, which is all part of the cyclical miracle of planet Earth.

If you find your bodily responses react from fear, send love to the body that is only trying to protect you – do not fight it, but find out why it is thus reacting. Love even at this level is the answer to fear, even in the primitive fight-or-flight response.

Just as love is all around you, so it is inside you, waiting

... all part of the cyclical miracle of planet Earth

to be born into knowledge and light. Self-knowledge which illuminates from within. So if love is all around you and inside you, what is there truly to fear?

Take all the time you need for your inward journey, for there is much to accomplish. Your body will prompt you if you start to lag. Indeed, it will drag you to the edge of your endurance if necessary, which is a hard but very precious loving act. Take heed of your body and remember it acts for you!

What if you do not take heed and plunge, or even throw yourself, into the abyss of darkness and despair? Take comfort in the knowledge that there is always a way back to the learning which you have not yet accomplished, even though it may not be in this lifetime. There is no escape from love! Can you not help smiling, sweet spirit, that love is truly the alpha and omega, the answer, the all and everything? Can you not help weeping from such utter beauty of existence?

All this is within you as you journey inward, discovering that each fear, weakness, doubt, or difficulty is but a mere passage to the ultimate love-place. No wonder you can only discover so much at one time, or so much in one lifetime!

Do you fear you will be unable to breathe, or see around you as you journey inward? On the contrary, you will be able to take refuge inside yourself and find the answer to your life's meaning. In gentleness and joy will your soul reclaim itself, even as a lover greets a long lost beloved.

Never hesitate to look, to search inside. If you are unsure, all you need to do is ask the spirit world from whence you came. You will be guided, it is a truth! Listen, listen to every silent voice inside, every dream image and every fleeting manifestation of your senses. How else does the spirit world best communicate?

As you journey inward, be aware of others as they journey inward too. You will not lose each other. Indeed, there are so many ways you can help one another by even the smallest of gestures or the briefest of prayers. It is all love – and in the end, beloved spirit, you will understand in the very essence of your soul that love is all there is.

*

Do you not sense spirit calling – you who journey through so much of what you do not yet understand? Spirit is prompting, leading, and loving you gently to the wonderful place of love inside yourself.

Do you not sense spirit calling?

There are those whose knowledge of love is so limited and there are those whose knowledge of love resonates through their entire soul. So different and yet the same. All born from the love-place and all to return there when the love knowledge is whole.

Some know of love only in their head, or in their body, but soul love encompasses all love knowledge. Soul love is so vital and so heavenly! Who would be content with so little when the whole of love is yours for the asking?   Remember you are part of the whole and the whole is part of you.

So much love embraces your every moment – so much life renewal. It is there in your blood and tissue, it is there in the tiny place of planet Earth which you borrow for your comfort and sustainment and it is there in the universal skies of your existence.   Universal love – do not even those words alone fill you with wonder?

Universal love renewal, given so freely for you, beloved spirit. Never forget that every death means a further renewal – every end is only another beginning. Love renewal of the spirit is indeed the stairway to heaven – the love-place, which is your Home.

On your journey, remember always to give thanks for renewal, as every moment evolves into the destiny of the universe. Giving thanks is in itself an act of renewal, for as you acknowledge the gift of love, you cannot help but feel its blessing in your soul.

Offer yourself to the process of renewal, for you are a gift unto yourself and to others. You are such a source of love, an expression of love, a channel of love! Every loving thought or act will renew you and bring so many blessings to your heart, even as it blesses and renews other hearts.

Do you not sense spirit all around you on your journey, waiting with so much love and wisdom? Yet the wise among you are those who know they cannot possess wisdom, for to possess is to stultify, to impede and even to kill. All must be free. Freedom is wisdom and wisdom is freedom.

You, precious spirit, you must be free, just as you must allow your fellow travellers the freedom they need on their journey. However, if you should find yourself trapped in your lifetime (and there are so many traps), there is freedom inside you – remember your inward journey! It is impossible for anyone to take away the freedom of another's soul. Likewise, no one can take another's love, although they can receive it if it is freely given.

Freedom lives in your own heart and head. Freedom to love and freedom to go where your mind, your soul-feet, carry you. Go where you will and visit beautiful places in your dreams. Ask for what you need. Ask for dreams – ask for wisdom – ask for freedom – ask for love. So much is yours for the asking!

Indeed, the very act of asking is an act of love for yourself and the love-flow will already be in action – ready, always ready to renew you with invigorating aids for your journey, wherever it may lead you. There is no place where love is not.

Does not sensing spirit invigorate you, soul traveller? Does not renewal bless your every living moment? Travel on, beloved spirit, in the certainty that love stretches behind and ahead of you, to infinity and beyond.

*

Breathe in the climate of your surroundings on your journey – your heart's climate, your mind's climate, your body's climate and your soul's climate.

What is meant by your heart's climate? The emotions that are prevalent in your current existence even as they change from hour to hour, moment by moment.

Sometimes your heart's climate will be dense with clouds that would seem to threaten your well being. Do

Do not avoid such clouds …
welcome whatever they bring

not avoid such clouds – stand underneath them with arms outstretched and welcome whatever they bring. Sometimes their passing shadow will be enough to tell you what you need to know, but other times, their rain will nurture the seeds already sown in your soul and your understanding will flourish.

Use every aspect, every breath of change, and every half-perceived facet of your heart's climate. Regard your physical climate and equate it with your heart's climate – so many illustrations, analogies and insights can be construed from planet Earth.

Be thankful for the storms, as well as the beautiful days when love seems to flow from your heart as easily as the sun's rays come shining over the horizon like a blessing. Let your sun always shine, quietly and steadily, even when the skies are leaden and threatening. Remember how the physical sun is always there, simply obscured at times by what needs to be.

What of your mind's climate? Some would call this the *Zeitgeist*, or spirit of the times. Your mind exists amid the climate of current beliefs, social constructs, religions, science and literature – a cacophony of cultural influences which many are led to believe is all that matters.

You cannot help but be affected by the *Zeitgeist* of each existence, as everything changes and evolves, leading you to uncover deeper truths, deeper understandings, and deeper love.

You though, beloved spirit, know in the deep stillness of your being that your mind can create its own inner climate, by breathing in from the outside world through spiritual filters of love.

Some would seek to blame current disharmony on those whose lives have passed, while others would seek to blame those whose lives have not long begun. They do not yet realise how the blame itself is disharmony. All lives are journeys – all souls are microcosms of the whole. Never seek to blame, only seek to love.

What of your body's climate? Much is being learned at this time – many re-learnings of previous knowledge. Remember that every healing thought and act will have beneficial results throughout the planet. There is so much to heal, because there is so much to learn and internalise for the right-being of Earth.

For your own body's climate, listen to your intuition, to what you know is right for you. Seek to nurture your body for its optimum benefit, but remember that body imbalances will never harm your soul.

What of your soul's climate? That is for you to decide! On your journey, you have many choices – choices which will create your own soul's climate. Choose love! The love choice will surround you with vibrations to gladden your heart and uplift your spirit, so that you would give praise for every moment of your life, every colour of existence, every nuance of being, from the moment of conception to the moment when your journey ends and begins.

Do not try to shrink from the different climates you encounter, beloved spirit, for nothing exists that is not meant to be. Give thanks and send out love from your own heart's climate to enter and bless others' climates –

give praise for...
every colour of existence

for every single atom of love will help to harmonise infinity.

*

Be ready to receive, in humility and sometimes in great patience, all this life can give you. Remember how the journey is travelled on many different levels. Much is spoken of giving, but to receive in loving acceptance is in itself a gift and makes for a more direct route.

When necessary, draw the cloak of yourself around you – yourself, your greatest friend. The world will not stop turning without you, as you regain your inner peace! The world spins on just as you spin on, circles within circles. Nothing is ever truly still. Nothing stopped.

Nothing lost. Even when you might feel you have become stranded or abandoned, your inner journey continues. How you travel your inner journey is your gift to yourself and your most meaningful adventure.

Such an adventure! Adventures within adventures – when you think you have completed one, congratulate yourself for having arrived at the beginning of the next one. There will be time to play, but have you not heard how to play is to learn?

Some would say that life is all seriousness, sorrow, pain and death. Life, beloved spirit, is how you choose to perceive it. Trust and doubt, hope and despair – all are sides of the same coin, all belong in the same circle. The angle of the circle is your choice and your soul's gift.

If you are tired and feel your journey is old; that life is but survival and so many have travailed for so long for mere survival – then you choose a stony path. Life is never old! Life is fresh, its every moment a new-born experience of love's perception. If you cannot help but feel that life is stale, go to watch a sunrise. Raise your arms and open your heart to the sun, which is as old and new as life itself. Life that flows in you!

If you should stumble on your stony path, look at the place where you have stumbled and see what it has to say. What is its gift, what learning can you receive from it? Study the rock itself that caused your fall. Love the rock. Become one with the rock. Receive the rock's wisdom. Then pick yourself up with a smile of joy and continue into the light. There are so many rocks, beloved spirit – so many reasons to smile with joy, even as your bruises heal.

Do you need a passport for your great life adventure? Your heart is your passport and everyone has a heart. Everyone has a right to their own journey, regardless of their life role.

What of life roles? What of parents and children? These roles are transient – there are no such roles in the love-place. Take care not to become trapped by roles in your life's journey and never seek to bind another to your side for fear of loneliness, or emptiness, or pain.

Some life roles can indeed perpetuate much pain – but the pain is your current journey's route, which you have chosen. Remember that no one can truly damage your soul except yourself. It is all yours, beloved spirit – if only you knew what you hold in your hands, you would feel you had touched fingertips with the angels!

The life roles are circles within circles and the roles come and go – they ebb and flow. All is one. The parent helps the child to learn and the child helps the parent to learn. Such circles are radiant spheres of light. All the love each circle contains will never disappear, but will fuse and flow into other circles, until each and every circle is joined as one in the eternal sphere of love.

*

What would you seek on your journey, beloved spirit?

The safety of the sheltered cavern, or the freedom of the wild, unguarded hills? Would you rest your soul in the nearby fragrant flowered glade, or would you travel far and wide to discover all the strange and breathtaking sights and scenes you can?

The safety of the sheltered cavern

Whatever is your desire, the pathways of the soul are always your own choice. The pathways of your soul are never wrong, for they all lead in the end to the same destination, where your journey began.

Whether you choose to languish in the flowered glade, or walk until you drop, you breathe the same air – the same longing for the love-place calls to your soul from the earth where you sit and the distant mountain peaks to which you aspire.

So what of freedom? Does the desire to belong to nothing and no one burn in your being? Do you struggle to lay down the burdens you feel encumber you and hold you back from where you would go? Do you gaze at the horizon and wish yourself elsewhere, on an easier life route?

Such desire is a burden. It is like being in the midst of summer and saying, 'Ah, but winter is on its way' or being in the midst of winter and saying, 'This weather is cruel, if only it were summer.'

Indeed, the very desire for such freedom imprisons you. Dear spirit, you are already free, for your soul flies where it will. Your soul is your life-breath and the passage through life is a miracle of being. Let your soul fly – let your soul inhabit the spirit-lands of hope, faith and joy.

Let your soul sing a song of freedom as you sit in the flowered glade or struggle along the difficult pathways. Let your heart remember its birthplace, as your journey unfolds in all its glorious wisdom. Let your heart love both the familiar flowered glade and the unfamiliar distances.

As you evolve ever further into the blissful vibrations of being, you will understand that true freedom is yours. Freedom to explore, to believe, to understand, to give, to receive, to hope, to harmonise, to heal, to love. True freedom of spirit, deep within your self – you, the microcosm of the great freedom of infinity. True freedom is yours wherever and however you travel, beloved spirit. True freedom is yours forever.

*

Have you ever felt alone? You are never alone – you never have been alone and you never will be alone. You are one with all the universe and all the universe is one with you.

Do you not wonder about the hidden knowledge that washes up into your consciousness like fossils on the seashore? (Remember how often this happens after a storm!) Do you not delight in the stirrings of realisation that sparkle in your mind like sunlight filtering through treetops in a shaded wood? Have you never marvelled at the sudden breakthrough of understanding that illuminates your whole being like the sun rising above mountaintops? It is your connectedness with the universe, from its mountaintops to its deep oceans, from the beginning and end of all time, which allows all this to happen.

You are connected to all that exists, having entered this lifetime to learn. The learning is so often through love, pain and perceived aloneness, but you will return to the oneness like the rain returns to the sky. Those who embrace spirit knowledge in their lifetime will understand the separation is a temporary misperception that does not in truth exist.

Rejoice in your connectedness to all that exists. All that there is, exists – rejoice in it all! Even what may seem detrimental is a loving gift of potential learning.

In your mind, you hold the connectedness of the universe, but so much is still unconscious. Slowly it is being born into the collective conscious mind, which holds the key of understanding to unlock the portals of heaven – the heaven of the knowledge of universal love.

Planet Earth, to which you are intricately connected, showers you with so many blessings, from the day you were born and drew your first breath. Earth cannot help but give – every leaf, every flower, every grain of pollen

every leaf, every flower ...
is a gift of love

is a gift of love. Just consider the miracle of a seed and you will revere the selfless generosity of Earth. Sometimes for the sake of balance, it might seem that Earth is taking away, but the taking on one level is the giving on another level.

What feels more precious than the joy of communion with another spirit? To acknowledge such connectedness is an expression of acceptance and love – a true giving and receiving.

In this lifetime there may be times when separation would seem to have the upper hand, but remember that such perceived separation is only the other side of connectedness. Separation is necessary in order to understand connectedness, just as uniqueness is necessary to understand oneness.

Differences and similarities abound in the human condition. Bless each other's differences, as well as each other's similarities. Bless each other in moments of separation, as much as you bless each other in moments of connectedness.

Beloved spirit, in the inner freedom of your heart and mind, stretch outwards to feel the extent of your cosmic connection. Your spirit is one with the stars and the stones. You have heard the saying 'dust to dust', but indeed it is star to star and love to love. Only look into the eyes of a fellow spirit traveller to see the whole universe shining in wondrous love.

Love without end, beloved spirit, for the end is but the beginning.

Let your journey continue!